I AM NOT A
PROBLEM CHILD!

How A Seven Year Old Black Male Child
Fought Against Special Education Placement

Marquise Cormier

Published by:
Professional Publishing House
1425 West Manchester Ave., Ste. B
Los Angeles, CA 90047
323-750-3592
drrosie@aol.com

Cover Design: Clark Graphic Images
Third Printing November, 2020
10 9 8 7 6 5 4 3

ISBN 978-0-9719749-9-9

Publisher's note

For inquiries contact: drrosie@aol.com

Dedication

This is being dedicated to the almighty God that I serve and worship for blessing me so I can be a blessing to others.

Table Of Contents

Acknowledgments

To my mother, Charmaine. Thank you for not having an abortion when you found out you were pregnant with me. Also, thanks mama, for being a part of my life and supporting me in everything I do. I'm sure it's not easy catching the bus, sometimes when it's raining, especially with my other brothers and little sister just to hear me speak or participate in my sports.

To my dad, Kareem. Thank you for accepting me when you found out about me, and loving me enough to try to raise me even though you were only seventeen years old and didn't have the slightest idea how.

To my papa, Paul Jones and my grandma, Kenny Jones. Thank you for loving me so much that you are willing to keep me around and guide me in the right direction in spite of the fact that both of you are growing older. I am truly blessed being under your wings. That's why I feel like an eagle and believe I can fly.

To my grandma, Lillian. Thank you for your love and support, too.

To the staff at the East 60th Street Youth Center, Dona, Marisela, my godfather, Melvin and my uncle, Quentin. Thank you for putting up with me out of love, not just because you work for granny. All of you have always been there for me. Oh, I can't forget about Gustavo and Ricky, even though they don't work at the youth center anymore.

To my friend and "road dog," Errol (Poo Bear). I'll always remember the fun we have had together while on the football team and track team and when you sleep over.

5

To Ms. Brandee and Ms. Coleman, my kindergarten and first grade teachers. Thank you for giving it your best shot when I was in your classes. I hope each of you never regret the patience you had with me.

To my mentors, Bishop Kenneth C. Ulmer and Earvin "Magic" Johnson. Thank you for being the kind of man I want to grow up to be by leading by example.

To Mrs. Zyra McCloud, the CEO of my school, who is determined that I'm going to be successful no matter how angry I get when I can't have my way.

To my other grandparents, uncles, aunts, brothers, sister, godparents, cousins and everyone else who believes in me. Thank you so much. My prayer is that I will always make all of you proud of me.

Thanks to Ms. Melanie Polk, the publisher of the *LA Watts Times Newspaper*. I want to also thank Donald James, staff writer, who wrote a very good article that has opened many doors for me.

Thanks to Ms. Shirley Hawkins, a staff writer for the *Wave Newspaper,* for your interview and story about me. Also, I thank you for referring me to *Black Entertainment Television*. Many doors have been open to me because of you.

And finally, to everyone who has ever been misdiagnosed or labeled and has lost all hope in dreaming. May you be encouraged to pursue your dreams no matter how many obstacles seem to get in your way.

Love,

Marquise D. Cormier, "the Eagle,"
aka « Scoop ».

About the Author

My name is Marquise Cormier, I am an eight year old entrepreneur. I am the owner and CEO of "Unique Treasures." I gave my company that name because my grandma, Kenny Jones, always tells me I'm her unique treasure.

I sell unusual, sometimes one-of-a-kind products, such as collector dolls, beautiful scented and decorative candles, colored glass marbles, oriental hand fans, fancy fruit tasting lip gloss, pins that smell like roses, odd shape yoyos, giant pencils, beautiful scarves, LA Lakers headbands, school supplies, and various other unique products that adults and children can use or have fun with. I can really sell, too!

Also, I've written my first book, *"I Am Not A Problem Child!"* I attend Corporate Preparatory Technological Entrepreneur Academy in Inglewood, California. I am a resident of Los Angeles, California, and a proud member of Faithful Central Bible Church, with Bishop Kenneth C. Ulmer as my Pastor.

Introduction

It was Saturday morning, May 18, 2002, and I was up very early getting ready because I had been invited to speak to a youth group at church. This was also a very special day for me, because it was my 8th birthday. I started to sing "Happy Birthday to Me," real loud and became even more excited as I thought about what Magic Johnson had told me two months earlier. He said by the time I was ten years old, I would be a millionaire—I was only seven at the time. WOW! Imagine having someone that rich and famous predicting your future! The "man" himself! As I continued to get dressed, I thought to myself, "Now that I'm eight years old, that means I only have two more years before I am rich." I'll never forget his words!

I had been blessed to meet the Magic Man when I attended a small business seminar at the Hyatt Regency Hotel on March 19, 2002. I had seen a flyer with his picture on it saying that he was the keynote speaker. I couldn't wait to meet him! When I arrived the place was full. If he noticed me at all, he probably thought I was just a little kid there with my parents, because I was the only child there. It wasn't exactly the kind of event children would want to go to. But, I was there on a mission. Since I have my own business, I needed to get some tips from him on how to become as successful as he is.

During his presentation, he asked if anyone in the audience had any questions. Before I knew it, I had jumped up before hundreds of people and was standing at the microphone. When I introduced myself and said I had a business, it seemed like everybody in the room was shocked, even Magic. You should have seen the look on his face, especially after I said I wanted to be an icon like him. He didn't know that he is one of my mentors. I believe one day we will become business partners. That's one of my dreams, too. After I finished speaking, he looked me straight in the face and said, "Young man, by the time you're ten years old, you will be a millionaire." Like I said, I'll never forget those words!

Mislabeled and Misdiagnosed

Who would have ever thought that I would have my own business at age seven! I remember last year, while attending public school, I had been labeled as a very aggressive and disruptive kid who lacked self-control. Sometimes I would cry for what seemed like hours, because I really missed Ms. Brandee, my kindergarten teacher, and I would wander throughout the school (after walking out of class without permission) to see if she had come back to teach at this school. She had left and I didn't know where she was. I felt like she was the only person who cared for me at this school, and she was always finding things for me to do to keep busy.

Chapter 1

The Public Education System Could Have Destroyed Me!

I was now in the first grade but I was reading on a 4th or 5th grade level, and boy could I do math! Everything was so easy to me. Somehow, as much as I stayed in trouble, no one realized that I was seriously bored there. If I finished my work before my classmates, there was usually nothing else for me to do, so I would start to act out. Finally, after many trips to the principal's office, they decided I should be tested or, perhaps, put on some type of medication cause they felt I was a disaster waiting to happen.

I was a wreck. They said my behavior was so bad that I should be placed in a special education class. When I overheard them say that I panicked. I couldn't wait to tell my granny. When they gave me some papers to take home, I asked her to please don't sign them or let my parents sign them. I said, "I'm special all right, but not like they think I am." Well, I told the right person, cause my granny was not feeling that. She freaked out at the idea of my possibly being placed in a special education class.

Then she did what I expected her to do. She dealt with the problem immediately. Granny was so upset with that school that she had me checked out by two psychologists, from the Children's Collective Inc. She said, she had heard a lot about its director, Dr. Jackie Kimbrough, and she felt confident that this agency would be accurate in checking me out. Jennifer and Sonny were my two psychologists. I like them a lot because they were not just pretty faces, they were smart too. They knew how to get me to open up to them.

One day my granny decided to pick me up from school herself instead of having me picked up. I was still having therapy so I guess she wanted to find out if the shrinks were doing me any good. While she was talking with Ms. Coleman, my teacher, I noticed her book of inspirational poetry, *"Something For Every-body!,"* lying on the back seat of the car. Suddenly, I picked up the book and walked over and showed it to Ms. Coleman.

When she asked me if she could read it I said, "Sure, but you have to buy it first." I think I surprised both of them with that answer. Guess what! She bought it. Neither of us realized that this would be the first of many deals I would make, and that Ms. Coleman was my very first customer. Thank you, Ms. "C." Too bad we were at the end of the school year. As many headaches as I gave her, if she knew how easy it was for me to sell things, she probably would have kept me busy selling all kinds of stuff at school. She was sweet too, like Ms. Brandee.

Chapter 2

Life—Changing Events

By the time the school year had ended, something happened that would change my life forever. We had completed my therapy sessions and the results were now in. When granny received the letter from the psychologists, she started to cry she was so happy. She couldn't wait to take a copy of it to the school. It said that I was above average and that I was gifted. Imagine that, me, "gifted." Yet, the school had labeled me and treated me like I was abnormal. After that she checked me out of that public school and placed me at Corporate Preparatory Technological Entrepreneur Academy.

When the next school year started in September 2001 we were in for an even greater surprise. Those two psychologists were right on the money. When I was six, I had taken the Stanford 9 test in April. However, when the school year ended, we still had not gotten the results back. It was now the end of August and they had finally been mailed to the house. When granny opened the envelope she was in for another shock. It showed that I had scored in the 98/99 percentile nationally. I was above average in every area I was tested in.

As I settled into my new school, Mrs. McCloud, the CEO, told my grandma that she was extremely overwhelmed when I told her how I sold her book to my teacher. She said that since her school focused on young people becoming entrepreneurs, she felt I might be interested in participating in the annual Black Business Expo that would be held at the convention center at the end of September.

She said she felt it was an excellent opportunity for me to use my sales skills and make some money. That was all I needed to hear. I asked granny if she would loan me some money to get a booth and buy some products so I could take part in this event. Again, as I expected, she was more than willing.

Once we arrived and my friend Dona had set up my table, I found out that I was the youngest person there with a business. Boy, was I happy! No competition! I got busy. I was so excited that I started running all over the convention center grabbing people and actually bringing them to my booth. Granny was a wreck as I would disappear away from her. Thank God, I was never gone too long.

Chapter 3

My Beginning as an Entrepreneur

Business got so good that I hired two of my classmates, another seven year old and a twelve year old, to help me out. I was moving so fast I didn't even realize that the *LA Watts Times* booth was right next to mine and someone was watching me. I was having plenty of fun and making money at the same time. I must have made quite an impression because the next thing I knew, they were talking to my granny about interviewing me for their paper.

By the time the expo ended that Sunday, I had made enough money to pay my employees and reimburse granny for the booth, the products she had bought, the parking and the lunches. I even bought myself a pretty T-Shirt and had enough money left over to buy more products and open my business officially.

I will always be grateful to Ms. Melanie Polk, the publisher, and Mr. Tony Walton for featuring me in the *LA Watts Times*. Their reporter, Donald James, wrote a very good article that has opened many doors for me. Granny says that's what good writing can do for you. As a result of that article, I was invited to participate in an event sponsored by the Evan Leigh Foster Foundation on December 8, 2001, which was the beginning of my other career as a motivational speaker for young people.

Now that the expo was over, I needed a place to sell my new products. So, granny went to the Manchester Car Wash—where she has been going for years—and asked Ms. Lida and Shahin, the managers, if I could set up there. Then she gave them a copy of the *LA Watts Times*. They were very impressed with me and said I definitely could operate my business there at a good price. Free!

Chapter 4

The Beginning of my Motivational Speaking Career

Then a lady by the name of Ms. Shirley Hawkins contacted my granny and told her that she had also read about me in the *LA Watts Times*. She said she was a staff writer and wanted to know if she could interview me for the *WAVE Newspaper*. As a result of her column, we were contacted by Ms. Margaret Hardeman, a member of Robbins Memorial Church of God in Christ, and I was invited to speak on their youth day. I guess they really liked me because they invited me back and gave me an opportunity to sell my products after church. I made a lot of money that day, too.

Ms. Hawkins also referred *Black Entertainment Television* to me and I was interviewed by them on February 14, 2002 for a spotlight on their *Teen Summit Show*. This interview aired the Saturday before Easter Sunday. Since that time I've been invited to participate in other events as a motivational speaker, including school career days.

Sometimes when I go to speak I don't even know myself what I might end up saying. Granny says I keep her nerves on pins and needles. I told her not to worry. Just go with the flow. You see, I like to be led by the Holy Spirit, that's why I don't like to write anything down and speak from a piece of paper. I don't want to sound like I'm making a speech. I want to get a message across. Like the time I was speaking to a 5th grade class at Loren Miller School during their Career Day. Before I finished I told them I was going to do a rendition of Martin Luther King's "I Have A Dream" speech. I stood on top of one of the desks, stretched out my arms, cleared my throat and with a deep voice (or as deep as I could get it) I said, "I have a dream that I'll never be a poor Black man!"

You should have seen the expression on my granny's face as I finished my version of the speech. I thought she was going to pass out in the classroom. Everybody was smiling, even the teacher, and when I finished it, they thought I was real cool and couldn't stop clapping. They even asked me to say it again. I probably would have but I had another classroom to go to.

I love speaking to young people about what it takes to become successful even while they are still young. I let them know they don't have to be a gangbanger or do stupid negative things to get attention. My granny says people are sometimes watching you even when you don't realize they are. Remember when I said I didn't know someone from a newspaper was watching me?

I also tell them not to always depend on their parents or guardians for everything. They should try to earn their own money to buy some of the things they want, but do it the honest way. When I was seven years old, I bought my own 19" color television and I even put cable in my room with the money I had made from my business. I used to have a real small black and white television. My papa was always hogging the big color TV and cable that was in the living room. So, it was always a problem if I wanted to see something in color or cable, especially "Toon Disney." By the way, since that time, I have upgraded my basic cable to digital cable.

Chapter 5

Paying My Own Way

My granny had said if I wanted cable that was fine with her, but I would have to have it installed and I would have to be responsible for the monthly bill also. To make sure I knew she meant business when she said I was to be responsible for my own bill, she had the cable turned on in my name.

For my 8th birthday, I bought my own Play Station II game and an extra controller. We saw it on sale and I asked granny if she would put it in lay-away for me. However, she made it very clear to me that this was a loan and she expected every penny back. In order to have it by my birthday, I had to do a lot of selling.

The school I attend is a private school and we are responsible for purchasing our own books. I had to have 22 books this past year. You got it! I had to help with that financial responsibility too. That's all right though, cause my granny says this teaches me how to be independent as well as responsible.

Oh, I also have to give one-tenth of the money I make as my tithes. Granny says this is the most important investment I can make and I am also being obedient to God when I give.

Since I don't go around begging for everything, looks like someone is always giving me something.

My room looks like a mini Toys-R-Us and my closet is full of suits, slacks and other clothes. I even have Stacey Adams shoes to match some of my suits. After all, I am a businessman and I have to dress like a successful one.

Let me tell you about my future plans. I plan to be richer than Bill Gates, Donald Trump and Magic Johnson someday. In fact, I'm even going to buy some franchises like Magic. Who knows, we might even buy a chain of motels together.

Check this out! I'm also going to be a pastor one day. Every time my granny buys a video from church and I have a chance to watch it, I try to remember the sermons my pastor, Bishop Ulmer, preaches. Even when I go to church and hear him, I listen real close so I can remember what he said.

One day while I was speaking at a Career Day at a school, I found myself talking to students about "riding a donkey to your destiny." Pastor Ulmer had preached that message on Palm Sunday this year and as I listened to him, I was nearly blown away. It was the "Bomb!" I'm sure he would have been real shocked to learn that a seven year old kid had been listening so closely to what he was saying. I just had to remember that sermon. I really had to!

I never liked going to children's church because I prefer to hear my pastor. I'm glad my granny doesn't make me go there anymore. I only like the refreshments they give us little kids after service. Sometimes I would start to act up (I wouldn't stop crying) just so my granny would have to come and get me out and take me to the big church with her.

You know how I know I'm going to be a pastor? Granny says I'm anointed. God seems to talk to me and use me a lot. I love to pray and touch folk when they hurt and ask God to take the pain away. My granny says it's called "laying hands." Whatever! Anyway, people say that whenever I touch them and they are in pain, they feel better. I know my prayers work because last year my football team had been losing every game. When the coach finally let me pray one Sunday before game time, we won our very first game. We had been losing ever since the season started and the season was just about over.

I also plan to be a philanthropist and give to a lot of people, (especially the poor), to my church and to the youth center. I'm also going to give some scholarships to youths who want to go to college. I'll be able to give a lot because it will be easy for me to do so. After all, I'm going to be famous and rich! Everybody seems to be telling me that lately.

I have so much energy that I play Pop Warner Football and I am on a track team. When I get taller, I'll probably even play basketball. I already know how to slam dunk. I have a real busy schedule. My granny says as long as I keep busy I will be able to stay out of trouble. If I'm not working my business, or speaking somewhere, I'm into sports. I just ended my track season and my football practice will be starting up about mid-July.

Although I'm involved in a lot of things, my papa and granny make sure I understand the value of getting a good education. Good grades are a "must" in their home. No exceptions to the rule. So far, my GPA is 4.0 and I've just been promoted to the third grade. Mrs. McCloud says she plans to find me plenty of speaking engagements if I maintain good grades. Who knows, I might even end up doing commercials or in movies or something.

I remember when I was only about two years old, I went to the studio with my dad, who is a rapper, and the producer let me get in on one of his raps entitled *"Put the Gun Down."* Man, I was flowing! I'm always rapping. Maybe I'm a free style rapper like my dad. I guess I've never been bashful when it comes to being on a microphone in front of an audience.

A few years ago I remember going to a program my grandma Kenny's friend, Robert Gilmore, was having. He has this young choir called Psalms of Praise and I really wanted to be in it, but I wasn't old enough. Anyway, I had learned a lot of songs at my day care center, but there was one particular song that was my favorite. I was so glad Mr. Gilmore asked me to sing. I started performing like I was getting paid. I thought I was Kirk Franklin.

Chapter 6

My Dreams

I'm always dreaming big dreams, and not just while I'm sleeping either. Granny says nothing comes to a sleeper but a dream and sometimes they can be nightmares. I'm a visionary too, because I see myself being successful even when I'm not sleeping. I guess I just want to let folks see that it doesn't matter if I'm being raised in the "hood" in South Central Los Angeles, I can still be successful. Granny says my visions are from God. One day when we were setting up my business at the car wash it started to rain. I told my granny, "I'm going to have to buy a building soon, because when it rains, I can't make any money!"

When I have an opportunity to speak to young people I always tell them the reasons I'm so sure I'm going to be successful:

- I have faith and I trust God.
- I believe in myself and what I can do.
- I always think big.
- When it comes to handling my business, I definitely have my priorities in order.
- I stay focused on my dreams.
- I'm always trying to seek knowledge from experienced people. That's why I was so interested in going to the Small

Business Seminar to meet and talk to Magic Johnson. I always tell young people, "never let anyone, young or old, define who you are, what you will become, or how you will end up. Only God knows!"

I knew nothing was really wrong with me when I was in the first grade. I just didn't know how to articulate it. Thank God for my granny! If I had been placed in a special education class, who knows what might have happened to me by now. I know I would definitely have been rebellious.

Chapter 7

Gifted, But Not Perfect

By the way, please don't get the idea that I'm some perfect little kid. I still do some stupid things too. After all, I'm still just a child and I do get punished. One day, not too long ago, just before school ended for the summer vacation, I acted up in school. Mrs. McCloud was very upset with me and told me I had to do 1000 standards.

Granny made me start writing, "I will not disrespect anyone." When school ended on June 22nd, I had only done some of them. I thought I had it made for sure because school was now closed.

I couldn't wait to start my summer vacation. I started making all kinds of plans. I decided I would chill first because it had been a long hard year. Then I would have sleepovers so my friends and I could play my computer games and I would work my business on the weekends before I began football practice. But boy, was I in for a surprise! Papa and granny said I wasn't doing anything until I completed those standards.

They put together a schedule, handed me a tablet and told me to get busy. Here I was in the second week of my vacation and nothing had gone as I had planned. That's right, I had to finish them, all 1000. My hand still hurts. Granny says as soon as my school opens for summer school she is going to take them in. She says she doesn't care how smart I am, she will not have me become an educated brilliant fool. I don't know where she gets all of these little sayings, but she means every word she says. She is "no nonsense" and has zero tolerance when you don't use common sense. She says it's called "Mother Wit," or something like that.

Well, I guess it's time for me to end this book. Granny said my cable bill has come and is now due. So, it's time for me to go to work!

Hallelujah!

Chapter 8

Grandma Kenny's Reflections: The One Who Knows Me Best

Marquise D'Aris Cormier was born May 18, 1994, in Compton, California. His mother, Charmaine Jones, had originally named him Marquise D'Aris Cook. He is the middle child of five. He has three brothers, Larry, Michael, Tyree and a baby sister named Jade. His mother, after realizing that she should not have named him Cook because that was not his real father's last name, she contacted his biological father, Nyrobe Kareem Cormier, and told him that he had a son. This was quite a shock for all of us because my son was only seventeen years old and doing what all teenagers do at that age. Fatherhood was the last thing on his mind.

When Kareem and I first laid eyes on this little bundle of joy, only three months old, Kareem picked up Marquise, placed him very close to his face and said to me, "Mama, what do you think." I knew he was trying to see if the baby looked enough like him to, perhaps, really be his. I could only smile as I said to him, "Son, you have an arm or a leg in there somewhere!" That's all it took to convince him that this child could really be his. We immediately turned to his mother and asked her if she would be willing to let him spend some time with us so that he could get to know his father. Without any hesitation she agreed, and before you knew it, we were getting him every weekend. By the time he was a year old, he had come to live with us. I knew something was different about this baby because he was so intelligent, he was a very happy baby and he seemed to be alert and very independent.

Although Charmaine allowed Marquise to live with us, there was a definite understanding that she was not giving us her child and she reserved the right to get him whenever and keep him as long as she wanted to. With that final understanding we all agreed and he continues to reside in our home, even today.

When Marquise was four years old, I noticed that he would often get to himself and appear to be praying. Then, suddenly, he would be trying to preach. He would get up and go to the piano and even try to play and sing. It was as if he was holding his own church services. It was about that time that he had heard the story of how Kareem had recruited a friend from the youth center he played at when he was growing up and invited this friend to go to church with us. At age fourteen, Kareem went into the water with one of the pastors of the church and assisted in baptizing his friend. One day Marquise was in the bathtub getting ready for his bath. All of a sudden he yelled for his father to come into the bathroom. We thought he had slipped so we all ran into it. Marquise looked up, turned to his father and said, "Dad, baptize me now, like you did your friend when you were a teenager." At that very moment, Kareem grabbed him and did just what he asked him to do. That was quite an experience for all of us.

Marquise was very active at his pre-school and would lead the group in reciting the 23rd Psalm and the prayers they were taught. When he entered kindergarten, we noticed that he had learned how to spell "Cormier" and he would try to write it on all his paperwork. Finally, last year, as he entered the second grade, he told his dad, "I'm not a Cook, my brother is, so why do I have to use that name? I'm a Cormier like you so whatcha gonna do about it?" Since he had discussed this with me several times prior to telling his dad, I picked up the necessary paperwork for the name change and contacted

Charmaine who was more than willing to sign it. When Kareem finally told me what Marquise said and asked me what he should do, I pulled out the amendment form I had had for a while and said, "Sign here, son!" He also signed without hesitation. We are presently awaiting the new birth certificate that will read "Marquise D'Aris Cormier." Marquise is looking forward to that day. He adores his dad and tries to do everything like him.

Once you get to meet and know Marquise you will see that he really is unique. He never ceases to amaze you with the things he says or does. He is extremely outgoing, he can be very dogmatic, loves challenges and is highly competitive. In addition to excelling academically, he is quite an athlete. He plays both offense and defense for the Seminoles Football Team under the guidance of Coach Jeffery Applewhite, and he is a member of the Quiet Fire Track Team under the guidance of his Coaches Robert King and Steven Black. He runs the 100 M, the 200 M and the 4 x 1 relays. His vocabulary is very large for his age and he knows what a word means when he uses it. He has a photographic memory. He is—strong willed, and can be extremely stubborn.

But in spite of his strong qualities, he is very sensitive and his feelings are easily hurt. Marquise is very spiritual, emotional and affectionate. He is never embarrassed to pray in front of others whether they are young or not, or demonstrate his feelings whether he is angry, sad or happy, and he will shower you with kisses in a New York minute. He is so loving when he wants to be that he can melt your heart when he smiles at you with that deep dimple on his right cheek as he gives you a big hug.

On the other hand, he can drive you up a wall if you don't really know him or what he is about. He loves family, and if he had his way, we would all be living in one big house.

He attends Corporate Preparatory Technological Entrepreneur Academy, under the direction and instruction of Mrs. Zyra McCloud, Founder and CEO of the school, and Faithful Central Bible Church where he is proud to let you know that his pastor is Bishop Kenneth C. Ulmer. Both his school and church are located in Inglewood, California.

He is being sought after on a regular basis to give motivational talks to young people. He hires different young people from time to time and pays them a commission so they can see what it's like to have their own business. Just think, we are talking about a kid who might have easily been written off, based on a school's definition of who they thought he was, when the only thing wrong with him is that he is "Young, Gifted and Black!"

TO GOD BE THE GLORY!

Kenny R. Jones
(His granny)

Chapter 9

Picture Stories of My Journey

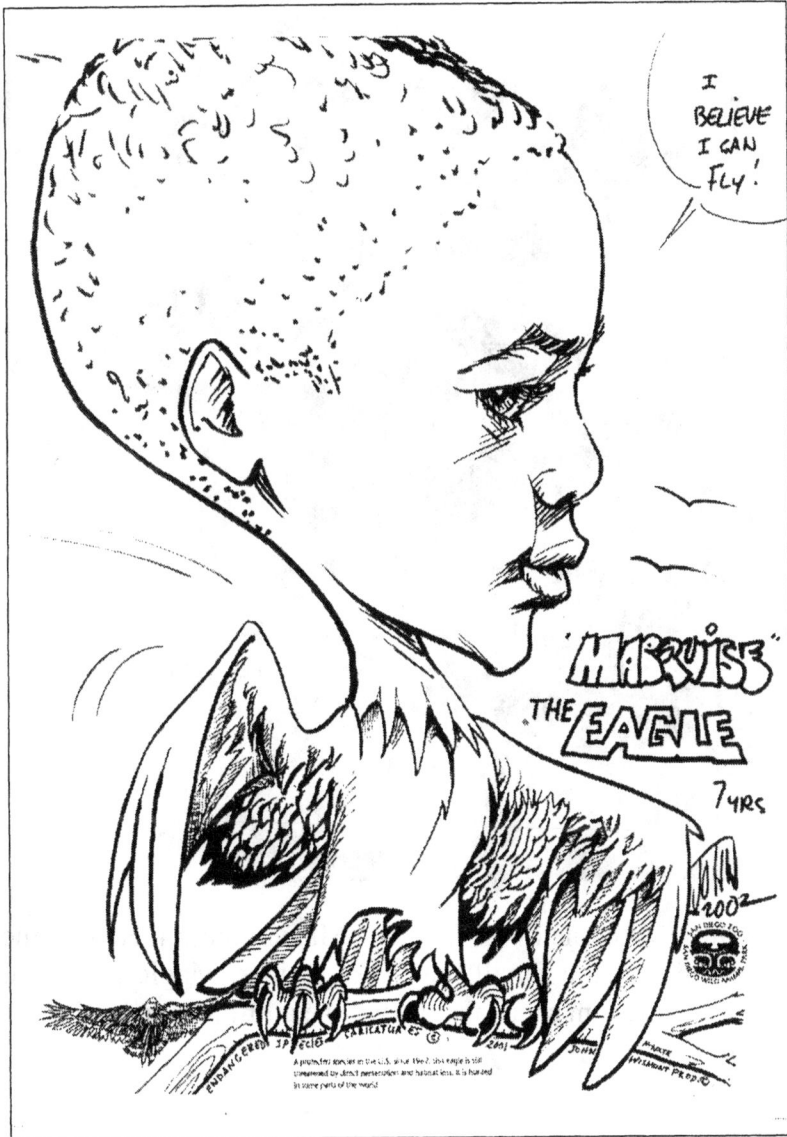

Marquise with one of his mentors, Magic Johnson. He was the only child at the Small business seminar. Magic predicted after hearing him speak that he will be a Millionaire by the age of 10!

A very happy child

Marquise on his way to handle his business!
Check out his briefcase and his professional look!

Dressed to impress, career day!

Quiet fire team picture 2002

Running the 100 M

Team picture of Seminoles football team

Pictured with his granny, Kenny Jones, at her Class Reunion

Marquise did so well with his business that he bought himself a 19-inch color television with cable for his bedroom. Marquise made sure his cable was in his name and he pays his own bill!

Since the picture was taken he has now updated to Digital Cable!

Opening day of Unique Treasures at the Black Business Expo, September 2001! Marquise with his special friend Dona Brooks!

Boy was he sharp for Career Day! He was so popular that day that everyone wanted his autograph!

Marquise, his papa Paul and dad, Kareem.

Pictured with his mother Chalmaine.

Here he is with his friend, Errol. It's a big game day and they are ready for action!

The 2002 Business Exchange:
Tour For Success Small Business Seminar

Featuring Earvin "Magic" Johnson
CEO of Magic Johnson Enterprises
Tuesday, March 19, 2002
The Hyatt Regency Hotel, Los Angeles
711 South Hope Street
Downtown, Los Angeles, CA

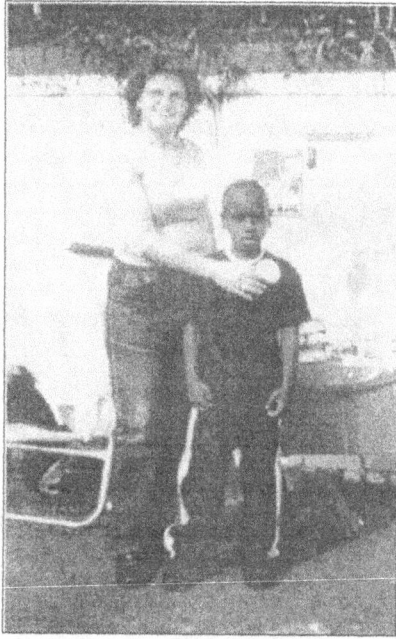

Marquise and Ms. Lida the manager of the car wash.

Marquise with customers

With his 15 year old cousin,
Krystal who worked for him that day.

Marquise pictured with Shahin, one of the managers
at the car wash and Curtis, a youth he hired that day.

Check him playing the drums.

"UNIQUE TREASURES"

MARQUISE CORMIER
FOUNDER/CEO
8 YEAR OLD ENTREPRENEUR

SHOP!

SHOP!

SHOP!

AT
MANCHESTER CAR WASH
1111 WEST MANCHESTER AVE.
LOS ANGELES, CALIFORNIA

For Additional Info.
323-231-4707
OR
Kenyspecialk@AOL.Com

47

I AM NOT A PROBLEM CHILD

STANFORD
ACHIEVEMENT TEST SERIES, NINTH EDITION

STAR PARENT REPORT
FOR
MARQUISE D COOK

Date of Birth: 03/18/94
Student No: 095   Gender: Male

SCHOOL: 1ST ST EL - 01095?
DISTRICT: LAUSD - 064751
TEST TYPE: MULTIPLE CHOICE

GRADE: ?
TEST DATE: 05/01

SUBTESTS AND TOTALS	Number of Items	Number Correct	National %ile	NATIONAL GRADE PERCENTILE RANKS
Total Reading	106	98	90	
Word Study Skills	36	33	87	
Word Reading	30	29	94	
Reading Comp.	40	36	85	
Total Mathematics	69	67	99	
Problem Solving	44	43	99	
Procedures	25	24	99	
Language	44	42	98	
Spelling	30	28	92	
Environment	40	DNA		
Listening	40	DNA		
Basic Battery	289	DNA		
Complete Battery	329	DNA		

CONTENT CLUSTERS	No. of Items	Number Correct	CONTENT CLUSTERS	No. of Items	Number Correct	CONTENT CLUSTERS	No. of Items	Number Correct
Word Study Skills			Mathematics: Procedures			Environment		
Structural Analysis	12	12	Number Facts	8	8	Earth & Space Science	5	DNA
Phonetic Analysis-Consonants	12	11	Comput./Symbolic Notation	11	10	Physical Science	5	DNA
Phonetic Analysis-Vowels	12	10	Computation in Context	6	6	Life Science	10	DNA
Reading Comprehension			Language			History	5	DNA
Two-Sentence Stories (Riddles)	5	5	Capitalization	7	7	Geography	5	DNA
Short Passages (Cloze)	15	15	Punctuation	7	7	Civics & Government	5	DNA
Short Passages w/Questions	20	16	Usage	6	6	Economics	5	DNA
Recreational	10	8	Sentence Structure	18	9	Listening		
Textual	5	4	Content and Organization	10	9	Vocabulary	10	DNA
Functional	5	4	Study Skills	6	6	Comprehension	38	DNA
Initial Understanding	9	7	Spelling			Recreational	14	DNA
Interpretation	11	9	Sight Words	5	4	Informational	8	DNA
Mathematics: Problem Solving			Phonetic Principles	18	18	Functional	8	DNA
Concepts: Whole No. Comput.	3	3	Structural Principles	7	6	Initial Understanding	14	DNA
Number Sense/Numeration	12	12				Interpretation	16	DNA
Geometry and Spatial Sense	5	5						
Measurement	8	8						
Statistics and Probability	5	5						
Fraction and Decimal Concepts	3	3						
Patterns & Relationships	5	4						
Problem-Solving Strategies	3	5						

CALIFORNIA CONTENT STANDARDS	No. of Items	Number Correct	CALIFORNIA CONTENT STANDARDS	No. of Items	Number Correct
Not Available at this Test Level			Not Available at this Test Level		

TO THE PARENT/GUARDIAN OF:
MARQUISE COOK
137 W 59TH ST
LOS ANGELES, CA 9005?

ADVANCED LEVEL/FORM: Primary 3/F
1995 NORMS: Spring   National

48

Corporate Preparatory Technological Entrepreneur Academy

101 N. La Brea Suite 605 Inglewood, CA 90301

2001-2002 1st Semester Report Card

Student Name: Marquise Cook
Grade Level: 2nd

Subject	Grade	Unit	Teacher - Ms. Jackson/Ms. Conto
Mathematics	A	5	Very Studious. Performing on a 3rd Grade Level in all Subjects
Reading	A	5	
Science	A	5	
Language Arts	A	5	
Handwriting	A	5	
History	A	5	
Arts/Craft	A	5	
Bible Study	A	5	
Entrepreneurship	A	5	Extremely Ambitious. Businessman in the making
Computer	A	5	

GPA = 4.0
Total Units = 45

49

Marquise was a motivational speaker for the school.

LOS ANGELES UNIFIED SCHOOL DISTRICT
Loren Miller Elementary School
830 W. 77th Street
Los Angeles, CA 90044
Telephone: (323) 753-4445   FAX: (323) 758-5081

Jean Davis-Mitchell, Principal   Sydnia McMillan, Assistant Principal

April 4, 2002

Dear Mr. Marquise Curmier

Thank you for volunteering to speak at Loren Miller Elementary School's Career Day on April 11, 2002. This letter is a follow up confirmation to a phone call, FAX, or letter you recently left us. The staff and students appreciate your interest in our school's career education. Students have been engaged in a variety of activities related to career awareness and your presence will enrich their experiences, extend their knowledge, and help them to plan for a worthwhile career in the future.

You have been scheduled to speak in the following classes:

Grade	Teacher	Room	Time
5	Bravo	36	12:25
1	Morcau/Aguilar	1	1:00
1	Bell	15	1:30
5	Reaves	35	2:00

Please make a concerted effort to be on time as we have a very tight schedule and the students really want to hear your entire presentation. Directions to the school are as follows: From the 110 Freeway, take the Florence exit and head west. Turn south (left) on Hoover (heading south for 6 blocks) and turn right on 78th street. Loren Miller is on the north side of the street. Please park on the school yard. READ THE PARKING SIGNS CAREFULLY AS YOU WILL GET A TICKET IF YOU PARK ANYWHERE DIRECTLY IN FRONT OF THE SCHOOL!!!!

50

LOS ANGELES UNIFIED SCHOOL DISTRICT
Request for Special Education Assessment

Complete this form if you wish to request an assessment to determine this student's eligibility for receiving special education and/or related services. Once you have completed this form, return it to the person designated below. Within 15 days, you will receive a written response. A student requesting an assessment should receive and complete the "Student Information Questionnaire." Please retain yellow copy of this form for your records.

Name of student (positive or initials) _Cook, Marquise_ Date of birth _5-18-94_

Address _177 W 59th St LA Ca 90003_ Phone _(213) 234-4966_

Sex _male_ Grade _1_ Student's primary language _English_

Area of residence ____ School of attendance _61st Street_

Name of parent/guardian _Nyrobe Cormier_

Parent/guardian address (if different than student) ____ Phone ____

Status of referring person _Classroom Teacher_

What is your relationship to this student? __ Mother __ Father __ Guardian __ Other (specify)

If this form comes from someone other than parent/guardian, is the parent/guardian aware of request? __ Yes _X_ No

State your concerns about this student: _Behavior, aggression, self injurious_
and to other students

PARENT/GUARDIAN ► I hereby request a special education assessment.

Signature ____ Date ____

IF DISTRICT STAFF MEMBER IS MAKING THE REQUEST: What prior actions/modifications have been taken to help this student?

Action/Modification:	Outcome:
Conference with Student	No Change in behavior
Contract with Teacher	No Change in behavior
Changed Classroom Seat	No Change in behavior

DISTRICT STAFF MEMBER ► I hereby request a special education assessment.

Signature ____ Position ____ Date ____

The school felt he should be in Special
Education Classes. Never thought he might
be gifted, that's why he acted up. He
was bored because he wasn't being
challenged.

51

APPLICATION TO AMEND A BIRTH RECORD—ACKNOWLEDGEMENT OF PATERNITY

USE BLACK INK
NO ERASURES, WHITEOUTS, OR ALTERATIONS
INSTRUCTIONS ON BACK

When a birth record is amended due to an acknowledgement of paternity, the original record is sealed and a new birth record is prepared.

A fee is required for the preparation of an amended birth record. This fee includes one certified copy of the newly prepared birth record. There is a fee for each additional certified copy.

Enclosed is the fee of $ _20.00_ for preparation of a new birth record and one certified copy.

Enclosed is the fee of $ _____ for an additional certified copy(ies) of the newly prepared birth record.

Jerry R. Jones, Sr.
Printed Name of Applicant
Charmaine Jones

_323 : 232-4966_
Area Code / Telephone Number

137 West 59th Street
Mailing Address of Applicant

Los Angeles City   _CA_ State   _90003_ Zip Code

ACKNOWLEDGEMENT OF PATERNITY

STATE REGISTRAR USE	STATE FILE NUMBER 1A	1B	1C

PART I — INFORMATION TO LOCATE RECORD—TYPE OR PRINT IN BLACK INK ONLY

NAME AS IT APPEARS ON RECORD

1A. NAME OF CHILD—FIRST (GIVEN)	1B. MIDDLE	1C. LAST (FAMILY)
Marquise	De'Aris	Cook

2. SEX	3. DATE OF BIRTH—MONTH, DAY, YEAR	4A. CITY OF OCCURRENCE	4B. COUNTY OF OCCURRENCE
M	May 18, 1994	Los Angeles	Los Angeles

ADDITIONAL INFORMATION TO LOCATE RECORD

5. PLACE OF BIRTH—NAME OF HOSPITAL OR FACILITY: California Hospital

8A. NAME OF FATHER—FIRST (GIVEN)	8B. MIDDLE	8C. LAST (FAMILY)
Michael	Wayne	Cook

7A. NAME OF MOTHER—FIRST (GIVEN)	7B. MIDDLE	7C. LAST (MAIDEN)
Charmaine	Denice	Jones

PART II — INFORMATION AS IT IS TO APPEAR ON NEW RECORD—NO ERASURES, WHITEOUTS, OR ALTERATIONS

NEW NAME OF CHILD

8A. NAME OF CHILD—FIRST (GIVEN)	8B. MIDDLE	8C. LAST (FAMILY)
Marquise	De'Aris	Cormier

NATURAL FATHER

9A. NAME OF FATHER—FIRST (GIVEN)	9B. MIDDLE	9C. LAST (FAMILY)
Nyrobe	Kareem	Cormier

10. STATE OF BIRTH	11. DATE OF BIRTH — MONTH / DAY / YEAR
California	10/24/77 October 24 77

NATURAL MOTHER

12A. NAME OF MOTHER—FIRST (GIVEN)	12B. MIDDLE	12C. LAST (MAIDEN)
Charmaine	Denice	Jones

13. STATE OF BIRTH	14. DATE OF BIRTH — MONTH / DAY / YEAR
California	February 28 72

PART III — AFFIDAVITS AND SIGNATURES OF THE NATURAL PARENTS

I CERTIFY UNDER PENALTY OF PERJURY THAT I AM THE NATURAL FATHER OF THE CHILD IDENTIFIED ABOVE.

USE BLACK INK ONLY

15A. SIGNATURE OF FATHER	15B. DATE SIGNED
X Nyrobe K Cormier	11/10/01

15C. ADDRESS—STREET AND NUMBER	15D. CITY	15E. STATE	15F. ZIP CODE
137 West 59th Street	Los Angeles	CA	90003

I CERTIFY UNDER PENALTY OF PERJURY THAT I AM THE NATURAL MOTHER OF THE CHILD IDENTIFIED ABOVE.

16A. SIGNATURE OF MOTHER	16B. DATE SIGNED
X _____	11/10/01

16C. ADDRESS—STREET AND NUMBER	16D. CITY	16E. STATE	16F. ZIP CODE
137 West 59th Street	Los Angeles	CA	90003

STATE REGISTRAR USE ONLY ►

17. OFFICE OF STATE REGISTRAR	18. DATE ACCEPTED FOR REGISTRATION

STATE OF CALIFORNIA, DEPARTMENT OF HEALTH SERVICES, OFFICE OF STATE REGISTRAR

VS 22 (REV. 4/96)
OSP 00 41300

CAREER DAY – Program
Saturday, May 18, 2002
9:30 AM

PRAYER / SONG
Min. Willie Harris

SOLO
Ashley Henderson

WELCOME
Yvonne Howard

SPEAKER
Marquise Cormier / Unique Treasures

SPEAKER
Felicia Riley / Boeing Engineer

KEY NOTE SPEAKER
Beverly White / Channel 4 News

FASHION SHOW
Steve & April Hill
Steve & Mary Bivens
Ever Renee Morgan

QUESTION & ANSWERS
Beverly White
Marquise Cormier
Felicia Riley

SPEAKER
Bernice Gaines / Operation Hope

CLOSING REMARKS
Yvonne Howard

"Shoot For The Stars – The Future Is Yours"

Seminoles 1ˢᵗ Annual Banquet

PROGRAM

Master of Ceremonies .... Malik James

Pledge Of Allegiance .... Caitlyn Lemle
.... La Precious Brewer

Invocation .... Marquise Cormier

Welcome .... Sinead Olivares

PRESENTATIONS

Mascot Cheerleaders .... Vanetta Smith & LaKeisha Williams
Co-Cheer Directors

Clinic Cheerleaders .... Vanetta Smith & LaKeisha Williams

Clinic Football Players .... Robert Summers, Head Coach

Tiny Mite Cheerleaders .... Vanetta Smith & LaKeisha Williams

Tiny Mite Football Players .... Glenn S. Deans, Head Coach

Mity Mite Cheerleaders .... Vanetta Smith & LaKeisha Williams

The Ernestine Williams Award . Vanetta Smith & LaKeisha Williams

Mity Mite Football Players ...... Jeffery D. Applewhite, Head Coach

ROBBINS MEMORIAL CHURCH
Of GOD IN CHRIST
3908 W 54TH ST
LOS ANGELES, CA 90043

DATE *1-28-02*   16-66-1220

PAY
TO THE
ORDER OF *Kenny R. Jones* $ *25.00*

Twenty Five no/00   DOLLARS

Bank of America.

For *Marquise Cormier / Youth speaker*   *E. Jean Hawkins*

⑂010102⑂ ⑃12⑁0006611⑂ 2154⑁310500

Sunday, January 27, 2002
YOUTH'S SUNDAY
Call to Worship

Prayer & Scripture

Praise Team

Announcements

Brieonna Dennis

PRESENTATION
Children Church and Sunshine Band

SELECTIONS

Robbins Memorial Youths Choir

"Unique Treasure"   Marquise Cormier

General/Mission Offering
Deacons

Spoken Word

Call to Discipleship

Benediction & Final Remarks
****

USHERS: Sis. Princella Harris   Sis. Ruth Burney
        Ireeon Bryson   Breanna Burgess
              Johnny Mayfield
NURSES UNIT: Sis. Helen Hamilt
****

Marquise spoke at this Church.

55

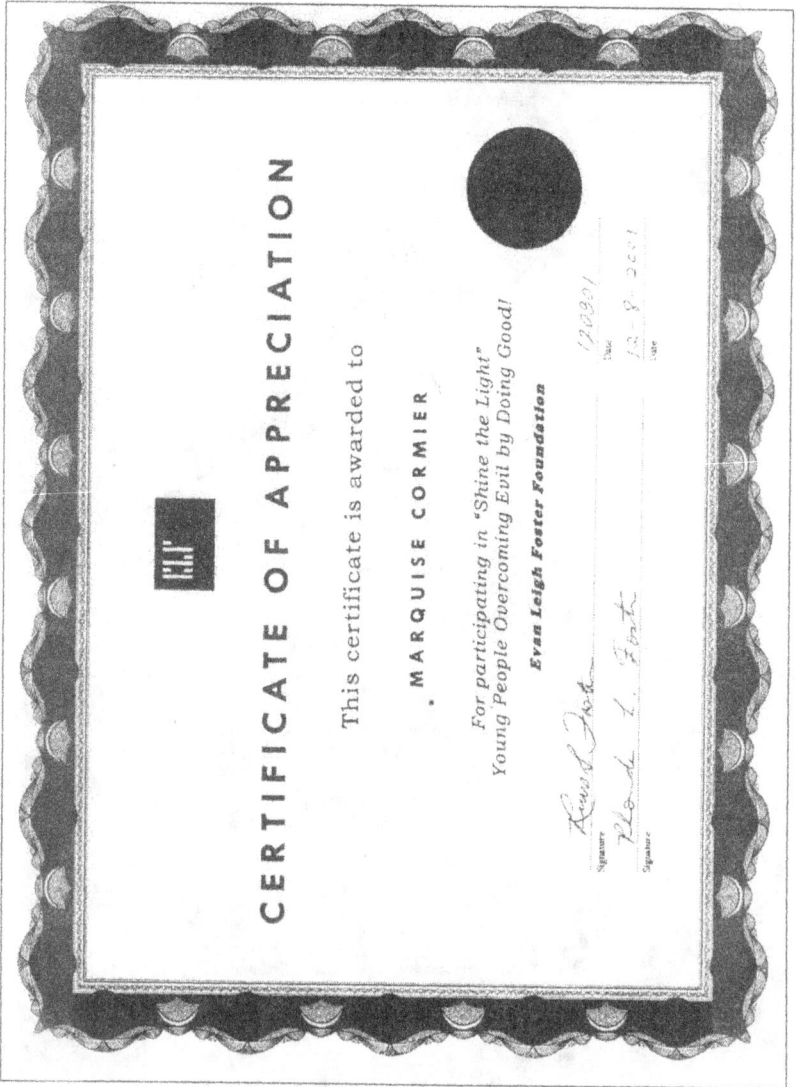

CERTIFICATE OF APPRECIATION

This certificate is awarded to

. MARQUISE CORMIER

For participating in "Shine the Light"
Young People Overcoming Evil by Doing Good!

Evan Leigh Foster Foundation

Signature

Signature

Date

Date

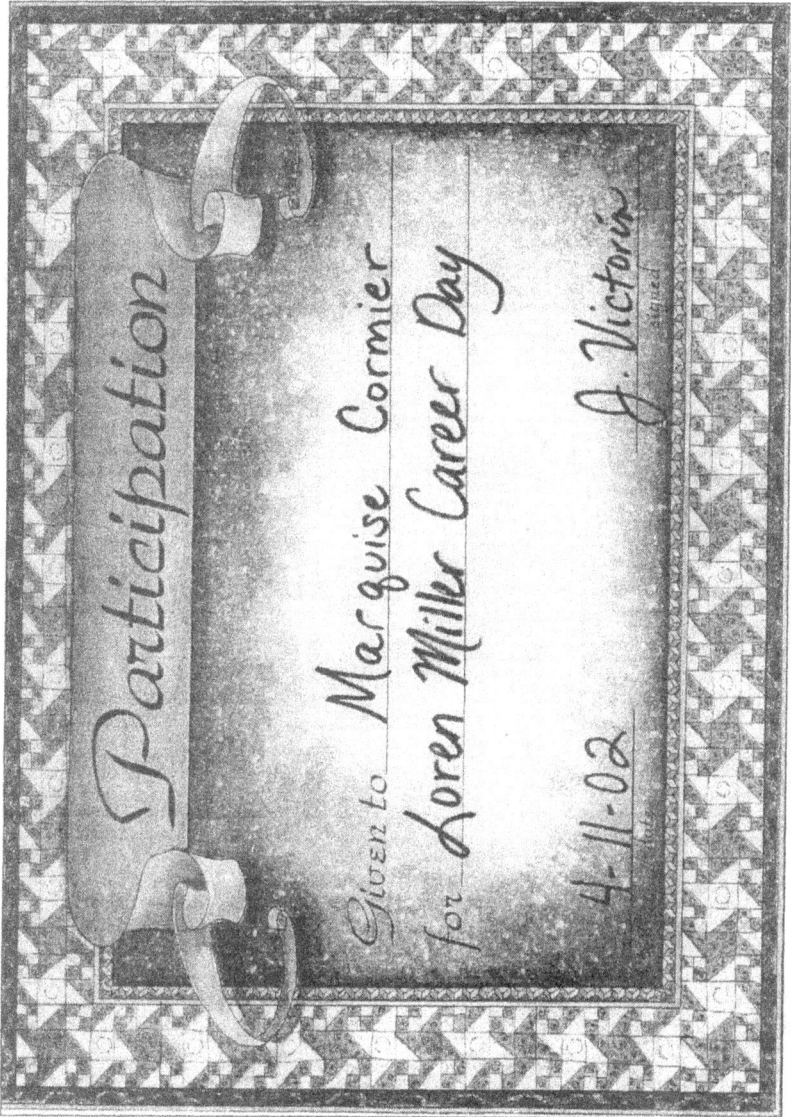

Participation

Given to Marquise Cormier

for Loren Miller Career Day

J. Victorin

4-11-02

L.A. Watts Times

Vol. XXIX, No. ??   SERVING LOS ANGELES AND SURROUNDING AREAS   October 18, 2001

BUSINESS

A Seven-Year-Old Unique Treasure Takes Care of Business

SEVEN-YEAR-OLD BUSINESS-MAN Marquise Cormier is the owner/founder of Unique Treasures. *See story on page 12.*

BY DONALD JAMES

LOS ANGELES—After talking with 7-year-old Marquise Cormier, it doesn't take long to realize that he is not your typical child. Oh, yes, he loves to play football and other games, much like many kids his age, but other than that, Cormier is in another zone. For one, the young man is the founder and president of Unique Treasures, a company that he, South Central Los Angeles native recently started.

"I sell all sorts of unique pens ... pens, exotic tops for churches and other unique items," said Cormier. "I also sell partnip items."

Cormier said that he launched his business several weeks ago, just prior to the beginning of the Los Angeles Black Expo and Trade Show, held at the downtown Los Angeles Convention Center. After deciding to venture in business, he promptly hired two associates, a second-grader and one fifth-grader, to work for him in his enterprise. Hand of brisk sales. And Cormier sales forecast was right, said, according to the young entrepreneur.

... were outstanding.

"I met a lot of nice people at the Black Expo," said Cormier. "I had fun selling things. People were just buying a lot of stuff from me. It was really busy!"

His grandmother, Kenny Ruth Jones, who Cormier called a business advisor, concurred with her grandson's assessment of business at the Expo.

"He is the kind of kid who says what he wants to do, and before you know it, he's doing it," Jones said. "However, I didn't know that he could sell things as well as he did to so many people at the Black Expo. What drew the attention of so many people was his aggressiveness and salesmanship. He was selling but among the people and bringing them back by the armful. People were so intrigued that they were buying his merchandise at a very fast pace. I was even mesmerized at what I saw he was doing."

A second-grader at the Corporate Preparatory Technological Entrepreneurial Academy in Inglewood, Cormier has a natural "gift of gab." He said that math is

See UNIQUE, page 13

UNIQUE

Continued from page 12

his favorite subject in school, and quickly speaks about his success on the pee-wee gridiron, where he plays nose guard and outside linebacker on defense and running back and wide receiver on offense.

"I knew that I would do well in sports because I have heart, speed and hands," Cormier said, matter-of-factly. "I am the captain of my team's defensive unit. I love playing football."

Though he loves sports, his goal is to become a businessman.

"I want to be a businessman," said the young man, without hesitation. "I want to make money so that I can have a better life. I want to buy a Fatburger franchise from Magic Johnson. I also want to become a pastor."

Cormier cited Johnson as his mentor. He also said that Bishop Kenneth C. Ulmer (the youngster's minister) of Faithful Central Bible Church was his role model.

Jones said that her grandson conducts her guidance in looking at numerous business options as a result of contacts made at the Black Expo. She said that several people including a vice president of a local bank and a college assurance, expressed strong interest in assisting the young entrepreneur. She explained that she is not pushing Marquise to do what he is doing. If anything, he pushes her to keep up with his business and sports endeavors.

While Jones is pleased at his grandson, Cormier is equally enthralled by her role in his life.

"My grandmother has taught me right from wrong," explained Cormier who lives with her and his father Nairobi Kareem Cormier. "She is right on time to talk, now to read, and she taught me about God."

For more information on Marquise Cormier's Unique Treasures call (323) 231-4707.

the
children's
collective, inc.

3817 So. San Pedro Street
Los Angeles, CA 90011
Tel: (323) 231-1367
Fax: (323) 231-6242

March 23, 2001

To Whom It May Concern:

This letter is regarding Marquise Cook. Marquise is a 6-year-old boy who was referred for testing due to concerns about his academic and behavioral performance at school. On February 16 and February 23, 2001, Marquise was tested for cognitive and achievement functioning. The achievement testing demonstrated that Marquise was significantly above average in several areas including: basic reading, mathematics reasoning, spelling, reading comprehension, listening comprehension, and oral expression. He demonstrated overall giftedness in the domains of reading, mathematics, and language. Furthermore, based on the results of the assessment and our knowledge and experience testing school-aged children in this community, his cognitive functioning is in the above average range.

Due to Marquise's above average scores in overall domains or reading, mathematics, and language, it is recommended that Marquise be placed in advanced or gifted classes in order to ensure that he is being challenged and that his level of learning is at the appropriate level for his abilities.

Sincerely,

Tressa Ferrier-Tucker, Ph.D.   Jennifer Johnston-Jones   Sonny Ray Ramirez
Licensed Psychologist   Psychology Intern   Psychology Intern

www.ingramcontent.com/pod-product-compliance
Lightning Source LLC
Chambersburg PA
CBHW060642280326
41933CB00012B/2115